The Silent Verses

The Silent Verses

Prasant Mohanty

Translated by
Dr. Sonali Sahu

BLACK EAGLE BOOKS
Dublin, USA | Bhubaneswar, India

Black Eagle Books
USA address:
7464 Wisdom Lane
Dublin, OH 43016

India address:
E/312, Trident Galaxy, Kalinga Nagar,
Bhubaneswar-751003, Odisha, India

E-mail: info@blackeaglebooks.org
Website: www.blackeaglebooks.org

First International Edition Published by
Black Eagle Books, 2025

THE SILENT VERSES
by Prasant Mohanty
Translated by Dr. Sonali Sahu

Original Copyright © Prasant Mohanty
Translation Copyright © Dr. Sonali Sahu

All rights reserved. No part of this publication may be reproduced, stored in a retrieval system, or transmitted, in any form or by any means, electronic, mechanical, photocopying, recording or otherwise without the prior permission of the publisher.

Cover & Interior Design: Ezy's Publication

ISBN- 978-1-64560-735-9 (Paperback)

Printed in the United States of America

Dedicated to my inspiration, the renowned Indian poet and Central Sahitya Akademi awardee, **Dr. Phani Mohanty,** *whose creative brilliance has been a guiding light in my journey. Your blessings, unwavering support, and quiet encouragement have given me the courage to believe in my words and to write from the soul.*

Translator's Note

It gives me immense joy to present The Silent Verses, a translated offering of the original Odia work Prasant Rubaiyat by the acclaimed poet Shri Prasant Mohanty. This book, a collection of fifty-five love duets, is more than just poetry—it is a tender, soul-stirring dialogue between two lovers, echoing their unspoken desires, silent aches, and passionate union.

Each verse, delicately carved, is drenched in emotion—ranging from yearning and surrender to spiritual oneness. As I translated these stanzas, I found myself not just interpreting words, but breathing into them the rhythm of another language, while striving to preserve their original fragrance.

The lovers in these verses transcend time and tradition, defy norms, and dissolve boundaries. Their intimacy is woven not merely through the physical, but through the metaphysical—through moonlight, memory, fire, rivers, and silence. They speak to each other through sensations, through metaphors, and often, through silence louder than sound.

This translation is my humble tribute—to love, to language, and most dearly, to the angelic presence of Silky, whose constant encouragement and squeaky cheer kept me connected to the beauty of literature and alive in its spirit.

May the silent verses speak to your heart as they did to mine.

Dr. Sonali Sahu
Translator

From The Poet's Heart

It gives me immense pleasure to share that my book Prasant Rubaiyat, a collection of love duets, has been translated into English by Dr. Sonali Sahu under the title "The Silent Verses". I am deeply grateful to her for her keen interest and dedication in bringing this work to a wider audience.

My heartfelt thanks also go to Mr. Satya Pattnaik, the esteemed publisher of Black Eagle Books, whose humble cooperation and belief in this book made its publication possible. His dedication to literature and his quiet encouragement have been the steady foundation beneath this creative journey.

1

Today's morning feels so rare, so new,
A wonder I never thought I'd view…
In soft grass where the dewdrops gleam,
I see your lovely face within the dream.

Is it a dream? I just can't tell,
A shadow of you upon my skin as well…
How, in the morning's dewy light,
My body stirs, warmed by the sun so bright?

2

It feels as if, long ago,
We must have met somewhere, somehow…
Otherwise, why, from the very first glance,
Has a new crease appeared upon my palm?

You're seeing me for the first time now,
Lost deep in thought…
While I am searching for you from a lifetime ago,
Hoping to find you again in this one.

3

In the hush of the sun's deep glow, a swing cradles a blooming flower,
Butterflies flit with trembling wings —
a fleeting, fragile shower.
Yet I can't seem to understand, don't know the reason why,
My soul is restless, tossed and torn, beneath the silent sky.

Your lips spoke the secrets of your soul,
Untangling knots that once took their toll.
Since that last spring, soaked in shyness and hue,
That flower bud has trembled — touched by you.

4

When a bud blossoms into a flower— it's the ghazal of love,
Whispers awaken softly in the ears from above.
Mischievous hues begin to stain the skin,
Seeping deep — in body, soul, and youthful sheen within.

I bathed my body in turmeric's golden stream,
Scarlet alta traced my feet like a dream.
Wrapped in blue silk, the dusk draped me whole,
And vermilion graced my parted soul.

5

In your eyes and lips, love's pollen lies,
A rainbow's shadow dances on your body
Such beauty — too divine to bear,
My heart has no room left to spare.

The breeze that brushes against your skin
Stirs a storm of longing deep within.
Where has the anklet from your feet slipped away?
I've searched and searched — night and day.

6

A thought lingered — unspoken, unsaid,
Fearing you might be angry instead.
I'm so tender, so quietly I burn,
Flames within me, with no return.

You never burned — not even a spark,
Yet left me smoldering in the dark.
There's no fault in this aching fire,
Just speak once — reveal desire.
Who longs for whom? Let the silence break,
Let truth arise for both our sake.

7

This sunlight — it stole something from your skin,
A warmth, a glow, soft and thin.
The sky now shimmers, scorched in that hue,
As if it heard the moon sing just for you.

Let the moon vanish from the sky above,
Still, the sea will rise — stirred by love.
This damp ache clings from foot to brow,
Since you've stayed distant... even till now.

8

Never let distance settle in your mind,
I'm the alta that graces your feet, so divine.
I still believe — one day I'll hear from you,
That ghazal of shyness, tender and true.

The dust of your feet — I mixed in my skin,
Hoping it would wash away all my pain within.
But in my search, you're never there,
Tell me, how shall I breathe this air?

9

In the dark, the morning smiles,
Holding a garland of blossoms.
You are that flower—
Soaked into my blood,
A part of me now, forever entwined.

Before thought could touch the present or the future,
The vermilion on your forehead slipped away—
The warmth of your chest in each breath I take,
My veil drew it in, as if claiming you.

10

Among all that is beautiful, you are the most divine.
Your eyes hold verses of untold grace.
The way you shyly glance—
> more beautiful than beauty itself.

Beneath your chest, a coin of love lies hidden,
> glowing in silence.

In a sweet dream, your silent face appears,
The crow's cry breaks my sleep like falling tears.
I wake with your warmth still on my skin,
Blushing softly, as if love just begin.

11

Though the sky has changed its shade a little,
My heart remains untouched, the same.
Across lifetimes, you are my only thought—
The moon in my dark night's name.

In life—or perhaps in death—I lie asleep,
Still wondering when that moment will be.
No longer hiding what my heart holds deep,
I've spoken through the tears that flow from me.

12

Your left eye, my dear, is a blooming lotus,
The right—like a lily, calm and divine.
I live in the emotion, high in the sky,
Yet never once touched what I call mine.

Now it feels as if you've touched me... without a touch,
As if even in closeness, you remained just out of reach.
Wearing the stain of love upon my brow,
I wish I could die—in that unspoken breach.

13

When I turned around, the ashes of yesterday still whispered your name...
That same uncertainty, like a shadow, kissed my feet again.
And in just two tomorrows, someone like you appeared in the mist...
Yet even then, love, a strange loneliness wraps around me—soft, aching, endless.

If I were truly meant for you,
Would you still remain so far away?
I'm soaked in you, like blood through every vein—
Longing, aching, burning for just a touch...
Living each day, yet dying a little more for you.

14

In the stream of sweat from your tender palm,
I now float—weightless, lost in your warmth.
Swaying in bliss, I dream with open eyes...
Tell me, love, why would I seek Kashi,
When salvation rests in your touch?

The Chaturdashi moon rises gently in the sky,
Its silver glow brushes my body and soul alike.
Why should I journey to sacred Srikhetra,
When you, my love, are my first and truest shrine?

15

The moon has risen in the eastern sky,
So breathtaking, it steals the night's sigh.
Yet all the beauty the world holds dear,
Is already woven in your body, my dear.

No one dares call a flower unlovely,
Its worth isn't lost for lacking fragrance.
Yet without that silent scent of longing,
Even beauty keeps its distance—untouched, unseen.

16

In the moonlight, blue waves softly kiss—
That beautiful navel of yours, a sacred bliss.
Drinking again and again from its tender well,
Even the moonlight fades... lost in your spell.

In the moon's soft glow, my body and soul dance,
Calling the darkness closer, in a silent trance.
Dreams are not enough for two hearts that yearn—
This hunger of loneliness… it aches, it burns.

17

A sword floats through the river of blood,
Fallen at the gates of a silent pyre.
History is etched not in victory alone,
But in the strength to fall—and still rise higher.

Let not the greed for power blind our way,
We are but fleeting mortals—dust and clay.
Forgetting caste and creed, we'll seek the heart,
And let love guide us, breath by breath, part by part.

18

I ask not for wine from an earthen pot,
For you yourself are the nectar I sought.
Your lips pour liquor, your eyes—pure wine,
Don't hold back, love… let all of you be mine.

After so many days, this sacred union blooms,
In silence, beneath the sky's quiet rooms.
Words escape me, caught in the heart's spin...
But one day, love, I will gather them—
And speak you into every line and hymn.

19

In the temple of your body,
intoxicated by the flames of dream's oil lamp,
Two souls, two breaths burn—yet I alone turn to ash.
And in that sacred fire of longing,
I carve a history... wordless, eternal.

This night has leapt across the bounds of seasons,
From far to near, we drift without reasons.
In this honey-soaked twilight, we wander and sway,
Every scent, every breeze... whispers only you, I say.

20

In the morning's golden light, the rose begins to bloom,
My soul is thrilled, my heart resumes.
For whom do you blossom, for whom this scent you sow?
Swear it now—just once—let me truly know.

That innocent age was lost long ago,
Yet I now stand where wisdom starts to grow.
In the dark of night, where truth begins to bloom,
You sing your song—softly lighting the gloom.

21

Your fragrance lingers in this basket of flowers,
Drifting through dreams on blue wave hours.
Let the moonlight reveal your tender grace—
And leave this night untouched, in its embrace.

This night will slowly fade into deep,
And I'll be lying in half-asleep.
In the silent language, I'll call your name,
From my feet to desire's quiet flame.

22

Even the blind hums, "Ago Madalasa,"
Soaked in the hues of Upendra's rasa.
That song—drenched in your sacred grace,
Shall make saints and sages drift through space.

In Kabisurya's song, I see the yearning Radha,
With Lalita, her faithful sakhi, beside her.
Soaked in tears, I ache like her in pain—
Yet through that ache… I see you again.

23

If the fruit of love is a hangman's noose,
I'll wear it gladly, without excuse.
Who else but you, in this world so wide,
Deserves the heart I hold inside?

You never gave me your heart to keep,
Yet carved deep lines in mine so deep.
Now each beat sings a silent pain,
An unseen blood that falls like rain.

24

If you take a step, I'll take one too,
Blushing veils may fall, but love feels true.
Let my trembling hand melt into yours,
Come, let's build a home where our forever pours.

In this simple truth, I stand helpless and still,
My body breathes the scent of a lotus thrill.
Alone, I burn as each petal unfolds in flame—
Where is my dark bee, the one I softly name?

25

Where your body casts its gentle shade,
Spring awakens, in blossoms arrayed.
The way you sit, with flowers in your braid,
Turns the earth to a jasmine-glade.

My life hangs softly in the arms of you,
I see no path, just love's quiet view.
Tears know not the way to walk alone,
How will these endless days be gone?

26

The moon of spring shines not like October's face,
But the one that made you faint holds a deeper grace.
That season's moon, where your eyes lost their way,
Is the dream I live in, night and day.

Every moon holds blue dewdrops in its light,
While fire burns deep in my chest each night.
It's you who burns within that flame I hide—
Then why ask me what I feel inside?

27

If there's anything called beauty in this world's name,
It's the blush of your body, a sacred flame.
Let me watch you closely, just once, so true—
Stay a little longer… let me breathe in you.

I'll stay here, just listening to your voice,
Even if the moonless night leaves no choice.
Alone, my shadow whispers in the dark,
And my heartbeat quickens with every spark.

28

Every moment, in your body and soul, I bloom,
Fragrance surrounds like spring in full plume.
Trees overflow with flowers, honey drips free,
And your lips are filled with a smile—because of me.

The April breeze whispers that you are near,
My chest blossoms wide with joy so clear.
With honeyed lips and eyes so blue with night,
How many hours must I spend without your light?

29

No one brought the other—love just found its way,
Two souls filled with longing, come what may.
Together we read that letter, eye to eye,
And made a small promise beneath the sky.

The night has turned so short, so strange its hue,
In what feeling did we meet—was it false or true?
What have I failed to hold or understand,
That you now drift away with a restless hand?

30

Come, let's speak to the moon as one tonight,
Then hide in the lap of clouds out of sight.
We'll sketch the key to life in secret art,
While stealing honey from time's quiet heart.

No time now to call the moon, my dear,
The night is fading, drawing near its rear.
Let the goosebumps of our union so true
Melt into the moon's body, like morning dew.

31

In the glow, you appear so beautifully bright,
Beneath that tiny mole, your chest holds light.
I'll search your navel for the blue-star's trace,
As warmth floods my body in your tender grace.

Perhaps I'll offer myself, with nothing to hide,
No hesitations, no secrets left inside.
If not, I'll cast my shyness far apart,
And gift you the treasure that's closest to my heart.

32

Darkness is born of thought, and so is light,
The world now smiles in feeling's gentle sight.
I'm learning to live, just learning to be,
As jasmine scents drift all around me, free.

I am not just a body — my soul breathes too,
I'm no flower bound to a lifeless tree's view.
To live within the bond of tender emotion,
You touched me once — in a dream's quiet ocean.

33

Cast off, my love, those jewels you wear,
Your body must be aching under their glare.
With open arms, I sit in silent plea—
Come, and dissolve your being into me.

Am I, or am I not, within myself—I no longer know,
I feel no will, no strength, no inner glow.
My body now drifts in your unbound hair,
As if someone pulls me, gently, from nowhere.

34

This moonlit night is not just for memories to keep,
It holds more than breath, more than dreams or sleep.
For the whole night's longing, for love's true play,
I've found you, my desire, in passion's sway.

The flower has now quietly wilted away,
Yet a strange fragrance in my body stays.
And when the moon hears the rest untold,
It will hide tomorrow beneath its fold.

35

Before the Konark of our bodies begins to fall,
Let us bind ourselves in love, once and for all.
In thirst between darkness and radiant light,
A river of longing will flow through the night.

The river of my life keeps flowing on,
While you drift in dreams, my boat, my song.
I am your melody, sweat beneath your chest,
In night's last journey, where silence finds rest.

36

The moon has faded in winter's cold breeze,
Yet desire roars, refusing to cease.
I tried to reason, again and again,
But this body still burns in untamed flame.

Why would I be angry—tell me, for what?
Just speak with care, with love in each thought.
Like sweet poison disguised as calm and clear,
I drink these waters of pain every day, my dear.

37

In the first rain, I'll cleanse the dust,
Your fairer glow will rise, I trust.
Even without the moon above,
Your beauty will shine, a radiant dove.

This earth is thrilled as the rain pours down,
The grass will turn a deeper crown.
In the dark, in this heavy rain's call,
How will I face tomorrow at all?

38

In my feelings, your passion will stay,
Adorned on my chest, come what may.
Braving the dark with a silent plea,
We'll search for each other in the rain's decree.

Soaked in rain, I searched for you,
In losing you, lost myself too.
Tears in my eyes now speak my name,
With no address, I roam in pain.

39

Within the beautiful, life is more divine,
But greater than that, your essence shines.
In that deep feeling, my poems arise,
I kiss each word in love's disguise.

Since our first meeting, you became my verse,
I still remember—that blessing, or curse.
Who was the fortunate thief, I wonder still,
Who stole you away on a writer's quill?

40

In the dark, you seem a mystic art,
By morning, a blooming flower's heart.
Beyond all dreams, you reign, my dear,
None can match you—far or near.

This body is made of blood and flesh,
Not a carved idol, nor frozen mesh.
As long as I live, I'll sing my tune,
Holding your body close, beneath the moon.

41

A blooming field brings the farmer delight,
Just as your earrings catch the light.
With every step and the sway of your hue,
My heart finds its home in the fabric of you.

No ornament shines more bright than you,
Even the Almighty crafts none so true.
Your strength outshines the finest gem—
Of this, I know, again and again.

42

As much as you can embrace the rainy night,
I'll come to you, through dark and fright.
Shivering in the downpour's tender bind,
This duet of souls—a beauty undefined.

What this poison is, I do not know,
It burns within me, a fiery glow.
Without love's taste to make it right,
My life is veiled in longing's smoke and night.

43

I know this night will never return again,
On its bed, life's flower feels the rain.
Yet we will soak, time after time,
In love's downpour, beyond all rhyme.

I know this night will not return once more,
And still, you stay so far ashore.
What feeling shall I use to calm my soul,
When tears fall like soap, beyond control?

44

The rain's whisper drives me wild,
Like school bells calling a restless child.
But I hear no anklet's gentle sound—
Why do you make my thirst unbound?

Darkness is everywhere, even home's out of sight,
In this deep shadow, we fade from light.
But let it grow darker—I won't fear the steep,
If you hold me close in your arms so deep.

45

Before your touch, the fabric slipped away,
You didn't pull, yet made me sway.
Holding me close in a breathless embrace,
Why do you ask—when answers trace my face?

I feel the warmth of my body melt into yours,
Like fire flowing through secret doors.
Let this night not die, let the heat remain,
Let the stairs of passion rise again.

46

Morning dew falls gently on my skin,
The cold creeps in, softly within.
But how can I shiver, with you so near—
My hand rests warm on your body, dear.

Tossing and turning, I'm pendiculating,
Sleep escapes—no signs of sedating.
Amidst the dewdrops, soft and wet,
How does sweat fall from your chest yet?

47

A devil's spell, cast in a black magician's chant,
You know it all—yet never recant.
You take my body, leave me undone,
This helplessness—where can I run?

This night sleeps in a strange disguise,
Half in knowing, half in lies.
Desires replay their shadowy game—
None as intense, as full, as your name.

48

Such romance blooms from your soft "unhh" sound,
A melody I'd never before found.
Now you've come closer, love's colors unfurled,
Drawing rangoli in the heart of my world.

Your playful words, like honeyed rain,
I've adorned them on my chest with pain.
At the end of dreams, in tearful flame,
They burn each night—yet speak your name.

49

This pathshala, in history's grand frame,
Holds us as a paragraph without name.
In the tale of night, I've offered my part,
Dedicated to you—for tomorrow's start.

In my eyes, you dwell—a spellbound gaze,
The hope of lifetimes, in love's quiet blaze.
Desire overwhelms, in shyness I fall,
I fail to adorn your hair at all.

50

Why do you adorn this lovely forest, my dear,
While night sleeps softly, so close and near?
Thoughts stayed unspoken, lost in the air—
Please don't leave me, stay if you care.

How do you drift so far from feeling's shore,
When you're the one my soul longs for?
I stay awake with hope in the sun's first gleam—
Swear on my love, say you're still in my dream.

51

I've turned silent, speaking my heart's true tone,
My touch will meet your chest alone.
We'll turn our dreams to living art,
In endless hues, soul to heart.

Perhaps it's written in life's silent thread,
Who can deny what fate has said?
A body seeks body, it's nature's spin,
But my soul craves love, day and night within.

52

You bloom and spread your scent in air,
A smile even in thorns you wear.
Why would I dream of heaven above?
This earth is divine—with your love.

You're a son of the soil, and I—a daughter of clay,
My home lies where grass gardens sway.
I whispered your name before dusk could descend,
And struck a note in the river that had no end.

53

Heart and body now blend as one,
Half man, half woman—where lines are none.
No scripture holds this love in frame,
As night ascends, it deepens the flame.

Night by night, like passion's grace,
You feel like you—yet fill every space.
I cradle the wilted moon on my chest,
And watch life unfold on a path freshly blessed.

54

The night my soul was longing to find,
Was your gift—so tender, so kind.
Even if morning comes, even if you drift away,
Without you, love, it won't feel like day.

In the moonlight of old songs, you're a melody anew,
A tune meant to last my whole life through.
Its rhythm echoes deep in my heart's core,
For I'm your lazy river, flowing forevermore.

55

In September's morning, my body softly shivers,
Yet I bask in the fire that gently delivers.
How this evening so tenderly soaks my skin—
With the blue moon's flame burning deep within.

How much coolness hides in your fiery skin—
Only one who feels, knows from within.
Two bodies now woven into one soul,
Crafting a rangoli of love, complete and whole.

Black Eagle Books

www.blackeaglebooks.org
info@blackeaglebooks.org

Black Eagle Books, an independent publisher, was founded as a nonprofit organization in April, 2019. It is our mission to connect and engage the Indian diaspora and the world at large with the best of works of world literature published on a collaborative platform, with special emphasis on foregrounding Contemporary Classics and New Writing.

www.ingramcontent.com/pod-product-compliance
Lightning Source LLC
Chambersburg PA
CBHW030535080526
44585CB00014B/954